"SO, YOU'RE ENGAGED?"

An Inspirational Wedding Planning Guide

By: TANIA A. WHITE

DEDICATION

This book is dedicated to the memory of my grandparents, Herman and Erma Smith. It is because of my Grandmother Erma, that I have a relationship with God, and it is because of my Grandpa Herman, that I truly know how to praise God through my suffering.

ACKNOWLEDGMENTS

I first want to say . . . Glory to God!!! It is because of God that I was able to write this book. God gave me the strength and the insight to make this book what it has become. I thank my husband, Maurice White, for standing by my side and supporting all that God has given me to do. Maurice, thank you for your support, love and encouragement. If I had to do it all over again, I WOULD! You can't imagine how your support and love has helped me during this time; you are the best!!! I love you and thank God for you.

There are a lot of people who stood in prayer with me as I worked on this project, and to them I say, THANK YOU. I thank God for you, Shirlene Martin and Christine Smith. You were the first people to give me a financial gift as I pursued the vision that God gave to me. I speak blessings upon your life, and know that you shall get a great return for your seed sown. Mom and Dad, THANK YOU! You have always supported and encouraged me in my goals, and I greatly appreciate you. Your continuous support has allowed me to achieve great success. There are no words that can express my gratitude to you.

CONTENTS

Page

INTRODUCTION

Hello beautiful!! YES, I said BEAUTIFUL. You are beautifully and wondrously made. Before you begin to read about the experiences and revelations that I have encountered, you need to know something. You are you, and only you can be you. Your wedding should not be what everyone else wants, but rather what you want. God made you especially for your fiancé, and no woman can ever take your place. Therefore, don't worry if you don't look like someone else or if you are not a certain size. You are perfect in God's eyesight. Do not allow others' thoughts or images of *you* to become *you*, but allow God's will for *you* to overtake *you* and change *you*. I pray that your fiancé is the one that God has ordained for *you*. I speak that if God has not brought the two of you together, that He reveals it unto you and that you are receptive and obedient to His will. I bind every attack of the enemy on your mind, body, and soul. I cancel every attack of the enemy on your finances, your marriage, your relationships and every business encounter you shall have. I speak the favor of the Lord over your life and every decision you shall make regarding your wedding. I decree that your ears are open to hear, and that your heart is open to receive all that God has for you. I will tell you as it was once told to me, "You are a designer's original." You are made exactly how God wants you to be. So, thank God for how He made you and understand that God did not make any mistakes. No other woman in the world looks exactly like you. So, do not compare yourself to any one else, and do not compare your wedding to that of anyone else. Allow God to make your wedding the way He wants it to be. My prayer for you is that as you read this book, God will speak to you regarding your wedding and all of the details thereof. I hope you realize that God is about to do something tremendous in your life. It is not for you to be frustrated, angered, or even confused, but for you to accept and get ready for the miracle and awesome blessing that is in store for you. Be blessed!!!

Tania White

Section One

your wedding. When God's will is done, the need for stress and worry is alleviated.

> **PERSONAL INSIGHT:** I was asked by the love of my life to be his wife on January 18, 2002. Of course I accepted, and in my overwhelming excitement, the next morning I began calling friends giving them the great news. However, I neglected to call on the Lord for direction in my conversations. I enthusiastically, asked my friends to be by my side on my big day. As the days passed, I made decisions of who was going to be in my wedding based upon what I felt and knew about them — with emphasis on what I felt. You see, although it was my wedding, it should never have been about what I felt I wanted, but rather, it should have been about what God wanted for me. It is okay to have a desire for your wedding, but allow your desire to work in accordance with His. I neglected to ask God to direct me to the women whom should stand by my side. The results of my non-acknowledgment of God were:

- A friend of 18 years dropping out of my life and wedding, with not so much as a call to say "bye."

- A friend who sowed seeds of discord among others, while all the time smiling in my face and proclaiming, "I've got your back."

Had I asked God for direction, He might have placed others on my heart to share in my wedding. Now don't get me wrong, some things we have to endure in order to get to the desired place where God wants us. When we encounter problems we are strengthened by them. By asking God for His direction and guidance, we can avoid unnecessary hurt. However, should God direct the decisions we make, and we still encounter issues, then we should realize that the encounter was purposed for a reason and will strengthen us in some area.

Have you taken the time to ask God for His direction?

It's never too late!!!

PAY ATTENTION TO THE SIGNS

As you begin to ask God for His direction in planning one of the most beautiful days of your life, you must remember that you have to *pay attention to the signs.* God will respond to your request for guidance, and He will direct your decisions while planning your wedding. God will begin to show you things, some of which you may not want to accept. Again, it is not about you; it is about God. God's will must be done in your life. God knows what is best for you, and He knows His desired end for your life. We have to understand and realize that God knew our end before our beginning. Before we existed, God established what and who we would be. We have to let God show us what He wants for us, not the other way around.

Do you remember when you first learned how to drive? You probably did not know anything about the rules of the road and procedures while driving. As a result, you depended on the knowledge of your driving instructor. The instructor had a desired end, which was for you to pass the driving test and get your license. It is the same with God. God is our instructor and in order for us to get to His desired-end for us, we have to listen and heed His instruction. God knows our situations and the conditions of the roads we travel. If we choose God's route and adhere to the rules of God's road for us, we will be successful in our endeavors. The same way you had to listen to the driving instructor to get vital information which led to your passing the driving test, is the same way you have to listen to God. God knows what we do not know, and by listening and being attentive we will not only gain valuable information, but we will also get closer to that desired-end.

There is no doubt a lot of tasks to be completed on this wedding planning journey. However, ask God about the route. One primary task is purchasing your wedding dress. As you begin to make arrangements and search the different bridal shops for that perfect dress, ask God to guide you. The bridal shop that you are thinking about may not be the bridal shop that God wants you to use.

> **PERSONAL INSIGHT:** I did not ask God for direction in choosing the bridal shop that would service my needs, but I found myself asking God to fix the problem. In my excitement to find the perfect dress for my bridesmaids and for myself, I looked in nearly every accessible shop and in numerous magazines. I was determined to find what I wanted. I found the cutest bridesmaid dress at

Bridal Shop A. The dress was $150, and required full payment before the order could be placed. My maid, matron and I decided that we would check Bridal Shop B instead. Lo and behold, we found the same dresses at Bridal Shop B. We were excited to find that Bridal Shop B only required 70% down. This was a little easier financially. Two days after the first bridesmaid was fitted and placed her order, I learned that Bridal Shop B had been in the news for providing horrible service. It was reported that Bridal Shop B was known for neglecting deadlines. There had been instances in which the dresses had come in the day before the wedding, leaving no time for alterations. Tragically, in some cases the dresses had even arrived after the wedding. Can you imagine the stress on that bride?! I did not want the same outcome, therefore; I took the precaution of calling Bridal Shop B and changed my wedding date to one month earlier in their system to ensure enough time to get the dresses and alterations before the wedding. However, it didn't stop there. I spent at least one hour every day calling to make sure nothing happened with my dress orders. I also went as far as lying and saying that I was one of my bridesmaids just to see if I would get a different answer.

Notice, I stressed and lied to make sure that all of my plans would be in order. I worried about the dress return date, and I misrepresented myself to see if I could catch the proprietors in a lie. As a woman of God, I went against God's Word. Going against the Word of God is a sign that you need to change directions. You may try to justify your actions by claiming that they served as a guard against flaws in your wedding. However, when we worry or stress about the things we say or display, we fail to trust that God can handle it. Of course, we prefer to think that we do these things out of our humanness, and we certainly do not want our trust of God to come into question. Well, let's make it plain.

Below, you will find a scenario. Visualize yourself in each example as you answer the question. Be truthful!

- You are a sixteen-year-old only child. Your parents have always been true to their word to give you whatever you wanted under certain conditions. Your parents would provide you with your heart's desires under two conditions:

    1. You obey their rules: no coming in after 10:00 p.m., clean your room, and wash the dishes.

    2. Do well in school, and get good grades.

You cleaned your room, washed the dishes, came in before 10:00 p.m. and you received great grades. So you inform your parents of your request. You inform your parents that you want the new MP3 Player and advise of the retailer with the best price. Knowing the character of your parents, and knowing that they keep their word, will you worry about receiving your request?

❑ Yes

❑ No

If you answered:

YES: You need to ask yourself "Why worry?" Your parents have always kept their word and you have held up your end of the bargain. If you still worry, then you need to get rid of some things. The first thing is DOUBT!! If you have followed the given instructions, then there is no need to doubt the outcome. God tells us to read His Word to get instructions. *"If you follow my instructions I will withhold no good thing from you,"* **(Psalm 84:11b NIV)**. You need to realize that if God says He will do it, then it is done. DON'T DOUBT, JUST DANCE! DANCE TO THE GLORY OF GOD.

If you answered:

NO: That's right. You should not worry. You know that your parents will keep their word, and so shall God. Since the beginning of time, God has performed all that He said He would. God is no shorter than His Word. One thing is always certain, and that is God's word. *"So shall my word be that goeth forth out of my mouth: it shall not return unto me void, but it shall accomplish that which I please, and it shall prosper in the thing whereto I sent it."* **(Isaiah 55:11)**.

So, if you have to stand on something, stand on the WORD!! The Word of God is the only thing that will help you, keep you, and encourage you. As you experience the trials and tribulations of planning a wedding, you can also experience the Joy and Serenity of God. All you need to do is acknowledge Him, and pay attention to the signs.

CONTINUE TO ACKNOWLEDGE HIM

Proverbs 3:6 says, *"In all thy ways acknowledge him, and he shall direct thy paths."* Through the planning of your wedding, you may be faced with opposition, and you may have to make some changes. No matter the changes, great or small, continue to acknowledge God. Changes could range from something as easy as changing your favors, to something more difficult such as replacing your Maid of Honor, who also happens to be your best friend of eighteen years. No matter the opposition, if you acknowledge God, He will direct your path. Webster's dictionary defines "acknowledgment" as, *"...the act of recognizing the authority or claims of the act of recognizing and answering, the act of expressing thanks for."* Acknowledging God means to make changes that recognize His authority over your life and continuing to do that which He requires of you. In addition, you will express thankfulness for all that is happening. By acknowledging God, you are showing that God is in control and that everything will work out for your good and His will. Acknowledge God in every step of your planning!!!

PERSONAL INSIGHT: In my excitement to plan the most beautiful and perfect wedding, I chose a young woman with whom I had been best friends since the third grade. Granted, others had come to form a sisterly bond with me, but this young lady was my first best friend. When we first met, we started out fighting each other, by the end of that year, we were best friends. Every family event we shared with each other. We spent so much time together that we began to look alike, and people actually thought we were twins. Try to imagine yourself having a similar relationship, only to have this friend drop off the earth in the middle of your wedding plans. One might be devastated, which is a normal reaction. Nevertheless, when you are led of the Lord and acknowledge Him in everything, you will quickly realize that God is at work.

Acknowledging God keeps you at peace and from responding in a way that you would later regret.

The Bible states that marriage is "honorable" **(Hebrew 13:4a)**. When your Boaz has found you, and your preparations have started, you have to be ready for the changes that God will make. God has to get you ready to be the wife that your husband needs. This may mean dissolving some relationships, including family. You must realize that your marriage will become part of your ministry. In order to go forth and minister the way that God has ordained and willed, you are going to have to get rid of some things. Once you have heard from God regarding the things that have to go, don't turn back. God will begin to tell you and show you the things in your life that must be eliminated. Making changes are not always an easy process, especially when it involves people you love. No matter the change, seek God and allow Him to guide you through the process. In the midst of your hurt, acknowledge Him. In the midst of your frustration, acknowledge Him. In the midst of everything, acknowledge Him. So, how do you know if you have acknowledged Him? Well, first you have to develop a listening ear.

DO YOU HEAR GOD TALKING?

As you plan and ask God for guidance, you need to make sure that you can hear God talking to you. It is imperative that you know and discern the voice of the Lord. The world says that when you get engaged, it is at that time that you begin to make arrangements and plan all the events leading to the wedding. However, spiritual preparations are needed as well. You have to plan how you are going to receive all God has for you in this new union. You must plan for this new role of help-meet that God has made you. You need to plan how much fasting to do, how often and from what. Yes, I said fasting. If you want to clearly hear from God, if you want a blessed marriage, and if you want to be able to handle all that is coming against you, you need to fast. You have to fast from some things in order to get through some things.

What is fasting? Fasting is a period of self-denial. There are different types of fasting that one can partake in. The Bible talks about several types of Fasting. A Fast can consist of denying yourself food, social activities, etc. You can fast for different lengths of time, 1 day, 3 days, 7 days, or even 40 days. You can allow Holy Spirit to select a time-frame within your Fasting days as well.

Know why you are fasting. Expect to receive results after the fast. There is a book by Elmer L. Towns entitled *Fasting for Spiritual Break Through.*

Isaiah 58:6 "Is not this the kind of fasting I have chosen: to loose the chains of injustice and untie the cords of the yoke, to set the oppressed free and break every yoke [of bondage]?"

<u>Warning</u>: The Fasts suggested … are not for everyone. Consult your physician before beginning. Expectant mothers, diabetics, and others with a history of medical problems can enter the spirit of fasting while remaining on essential diets. While fasting is healthful to many, the nature of God would not command a physical exercise that would harm people physically or emotionally. Be sure this is the Fasts God chooses.

Know that Fasting is not an end in itself; it is a means by which we can worship the Lord and submit ourselves in humility to Him.

1. The Disciple's Fast (Fasting for freedom from addiction (*see* Matthew 17:20, 21). If we fast, we can break the besetting sins that limit a life of freedom in Christ.)

2. The Ezra Fast (Fasting to solve problems (*see* Ezra 8:21-23). If we fast for a specific purpose, we may solve a debilitating problem.)

3. The Samuel Fast (Fasting to win people to Christ (*see* I Samuel 7:1-8). If we fast and pray for revival, God will pour Himself on His people.)

4. The Elijah Fast (Fasting to break crippling fears and other mental problems (*see* I Kings 19:2-18) Through fasting, God will show us how to overcome negative emotional and personal habits.)

5. The Widow's Fast (Fasting to provide for the needy (*see* I Kings 17:12). When we sacrifice our own physical needs, God enables us to focus on and provide for the needs of others.)

6. The [ ]Paul Fast (Fasting for insight and decision making (*see* Acts 9:9-19). If we fast to subject our will to God's, He will reveal His will to us.)

7. The Daniel Fast (Fasting for health and physical healing (*see* Daniel 1:12-20). When we fast for physical well-being, God will touch our bodies and enrich our souls.)

8. The John The Baptist Fast (Fasting for an influential testimony (*see* Matthew 3:4; Luke 1:15). If we fast for the influence of our testimonies, God will use us.)

9. The Esther Fast (Fasting for protection from the evil one (*see* Esther 4:16). If we fast for protection and deliverance from Satan, God will deliver us from evil.)*

Matthew 17:18-21

> 18*And Jesus rebuked the devil; and he departed out of him: and the child was cured from that very hour.* 19*Then came the disciples to Jesus apart, and said, Why could not we cast him out?* 20*And Jesus said unto them, Because of your unbelief: for verily I say unto you, If ye have faith as a grain of mustard seed, ye shall say unto this mountain, Remove hence to yonder place; and it shall remove; and nothing shall be impossible unto you.* 21*Howbeit this kind goeth not out but by <u>prayer and fasting</u>.*

What am I saying to you? During the course of this wedding planning you are going to have to rebuke some people and things. This is something you can't do in your natural mind. You may be faced with the need to rebuke the negativity and jealousy of family or friends. In fact, you may

---

* (Elmer L. Towns, *Fasting for Spiritual Break Through*. Ventura: Regal Books)

have to tell someone whose trying to block your blessing to remove hence to yonder place. In other words, "Get lost!" However, you cannot do this in your own strength. Some of us have a hard time with confrontations, especially if it is with a loved one or close friend. Only by the power of God can you rebuke the devil within them and move on to do what you have to do in Christ. When you fast and pray, God moves. The fact that you are denying yourself to obtain strength and guidance for His will, changes your outcome.

> **PERSONAL INSIGHT:** My fiancé and I fasted off and on from the moment we were engaged until the moment we said, "I do." We realized that the enemy hates marriage because it reminds him of Jesus and the church. We also knew that we would experience an attack like no other. I have heard horror stories surrounding wedding planning, friends and even family. I was determined not to experience a horror story like the ones I had heard. Now, you know I had no control over what God would allow to happen, but I had control over the outcome.
>
> During my wedding planning months, I experienced all that would, could, and should be considered a HORROR STORY. However, as a direct result of my fasting and prayers, the would-be horror story had a happy ending. Fasting and praying gives you strength unlike

anything you could ever experience. It affords you a comfort and inner peace. There were many things that happened during the planning of my wedding, but I will tell you about the one that touched me the most. Upon entering high school I met a young lady that lived close to me. This young lady and I created such a bond that we were more like sisters than friends. We, as well as others, formed our special little sister group with made up names to signify our unity. This young lady and I shared secrets over one another's dinner table, late night conversations about boys and our dreams and desires for the future. We attended separate Universities, but we were only a phone call and highway away. There were many days that I phoned her with tears in my eyes, and needing her support, and the same was true for her. Nothing kept us from being there for each other.

My friend had a desire to be a make-up artist, and she had the skills to be the best. Coupled with this God-given gift, my friend had a strong desire to make this a reality in her life. Through general conversation, she mentioned that she was going to take some make-up artist classes. I thought, "WOW! This is great. I think I can help her dream become a reality." It never occurred to me that the most important thing to her would be to stand by my side. In my mind I thought, "It's just a wedding, a one day event. I wanted to give her a gift that will last." I didn't look at this from a sister's eye or

God's eye as I had my own agenda. So, as a result, I never asked my friend to be in my wedding. I just told her that I had something important to talk to her about and that I needed to meet with her. It was my dream to give one of my best friends the best gift, her dream. I thought that as I experienced the most memorable time in my life, I could also help to make this a memorable time for her. My wedding was going to be a life-changing event for the two of us, or so I thought.

Again … I am thinking and not seeking God for guidance. My friend had a passion around a certain brand of make-up, so within this brand, I priced every size make-up brush, which totaled about $125. I then priced a makeup case for $250, along with some cleaning materials, and ordered 500 laminated business cards with the make-up artist symbol. My desire was to provide my friend with everything she needed for her own make-up business. It was my thought that this was the best gift that I could have given her for my wedding. We were unable to get our schedules together for dinner, so I informed her of the plans over the phone. She seemed fine with the details, at least for that moment. The plans were to provide my friend with everything she needed to get her business started, and my wedding would be her first paying job and serve as publicity. Not only did I buy everything, but I also agreed to pay $25 per face. I had eight girls plus myself, so you do the math. I thought that this was a seed I could sow into someone I loved. I thought I would be giving my friend the best. Well, after my friend discussed this with other individuals, she came to the conclusion that she did not want to be a part of my wedding. She felt that she was second-choice and that she was only needed to do the make-up. I was devastated to say the least. I explained my thoughts, my position and reiterated all that I had spent on her for my wedding. I told her that anyone in second place would not get what I was offering. I explained that it was my dream to help her achieve her dream by buying all of her supplies, paying her and promoting her business. Do you know what she said to me? She said, "I don't care, I don't want to be a part of it. Take back everything you bought, I don't want it." Imagine that!! To have said that I was hurt and angry would have been an understatement. We had shared a bond for twelve years, and I felt like it had been thrown in my face. My first reaction was to go off. But I remembered that God was there to keep me and to bridle my tongue. I remained humble and just hung up. Fasting and praying kept me that day. While my natural self wanted to say, "You selfish, no good, ungrateful....," God gave me the strength to merely say, "Okay." The fact is, I have peace concerning her and this issue. I looked for her at the wedding, but she didn't come. God still kept me. I can honestly say that if I had not fasted and prayed for strength, stood on His Word that told me that no weapon formed against me would prosper **(Isaiah 54:17a)**, I would have cursed her. That would have kept me from my blessings. What am I saying? I am saying that you are going to come up against some things that will shake you, and if you are not fasted and prayed up, you will crumble.

Pray for a hearing ear!!!

PROGRESSIVE INSIGHT: As I re-read this book that God has given me, I was overtaken with sadness after reading this section. I was so focused on blessing my friend the way "I thought" would be best, that I didn't realize what she really needed, or wanted.

When you are compelled to bless someone, always ask God how you should bless that person, and WAIT to hear what He has to say. Never be so focused on blessing that you miss the need of the person.

Makeup and money probably didn't matter to her, all she wanted was to stand by my side.

My misdirected focus hindered her blessing and mine. Thinking back…. I missed out on having my sister by my side all because I didn't seek and listen.

Friend, if you are reading this I AM SORRY for hurting you and not listening to provide you the blessing you needed, and not the one I wanted.

Please forgive me…. I love you!!!

KEEP GOD FIRST

No matter what changes have to be made with your friends, the wedding or your family, be sure to keep God first. *"In all thy ways; acknowledge him, and he shall direct thy paths"* **(Proverbs 3:6)**. Before you do anything, or plan anything, acknowledge Him. It is important that you keep God involved in all that you do. He must be first no matter what the situation or circumstance. As you plan your wedding, you will begin to see things that you want for your big day. If you acknowledge God and keep Him first, God will direct you to places where you can get the items you desire at a fraction of the cost.

One thing that my "fiancé" and I made sure to do before every discussion or meeting was to pray. We invited God into everything and allowed Him to lead us. This made every difference in the world. Because we kept God first, we were guided to stores with special discounts, reception halls with extra benefits, and people with special skills. God placed us in the path to be blessed and to experience a beautiful, elegant wedding.

PERSONAL INSIGHT: I began looking for places to reserve our reception. The prices for a Saturday reception was $30 minimum per plate with no cake included. My fiancé and I prayed for direction and asked God to guide us. About a day or so later my fiancé suggested that we look at some hotels. He thought that if we used a hotel we could probably get a better deal. The same day my mother called me at work and asked my thoughts on using the hotel a few miles from my home. I told her that my fiancé had suggested the same thing, and I asked her to get more information. God was already working. The hotel was in the process of building a new extension with ballrooms and a separate entrance. We thought this was a great opportunity. When we received the package of information, we were amazed at what was being offered. God led us to a hotel with newly remodeled ballrooms and chandeliers, a well known gourmet chef, a gourmet cake of our choice, style and size, hotel accommodations for the night of the wedding, next day brunch, a replica of our wedding cake for our one year anniversary, a hotel stay for our one year anniversary and a steak dinner for use at anytime. We only had to pay $26 per plate. Here it was, every other place wanted to charge $30 a plate, and we would have only received food for that night.

**WHEN GOD GUIDES YOU, HE GUIDES YOU TO THE BEST.
I DARE YOU TO TRY HIM.**

You have completed the first section of this spiritual insight to planning your wedding. It is my hope that you have been blessed thus far, and as you continue reading and interacting with this inspirational guide, you will be touched and led to allow God to be in control. Your wedding does not have to be stressful and full of tears. Through this book, God has allowed me to share my experiences, as well as things that will enhance not only your wedding but also your life. This will be a beautiful moment, and you are about to make a beautiful bride. Use the next sections for encouragement as you plan your God guided, stress free, and beautiful wedding. Relax, read your Word, pray and have some tea. God is about to do something awesome in you and through you.

Enjoy the next Sections, as they will provide you with:

- Scriptures to encourage you.

- Health tips to sustain you.

- Interactive journal to motivate you.

- Planning guide to direct you.

Section Two

SCRIPTURES TO STAND ON

As you plan your special day, there is something you need to have. You need to have *Scriptures To Stand On.* It is important for you to know who you are in God, and who you will be to your husband. On a daily basis, we, as women, deal with aspects of our health, having peace in our families, and joy in our lives. While planning your wedding, and your life thereafter, you will deal with these aspects, but you will also deal with money concerns. This section will give you scriptures that you can stand on when you are facing these circumstances. The first scripture you should know is what God says about His word. God says in **Isaiah 55:11**, *"So shall My word be that goes forth from My mouth; It shall not return to Me void, but it shall accomplish what I please, and it shall prosper in the thing for which I sent it."* (NIV) Through this scripture, God is telling you that every promise He made to you in His word will come to pass. Knowing this alone is something to shout about. Whatever God tells you He will do, you should consider it done. This scripture should be the foundation for the other scriptures that you will encounter throughout this book. God has allowed me to be His mouthpiece and provide you with scriptures to help you through your wedding planning and even your marriage.

Now that you have your foundation scripture, you need to know who you are in God.

Philippians 4:13: *I can do all things through Christ which strengtheneth me.*

Isaiah 54:17a: *No weapon that is formed against thee shall prosper; and every tongue that shall rise against thee in judgment thou shalt condemn...*

Proverbs 3:6: *In all thy ways acknowledge him, and he shall direct thy paths.*

There are more scriptures that you can stand on, however, I found that these three became my favorites. Be sure to ask God to give you scriptures as they relate to your situation.

Do you know how special you are? You are made in His image, and you are an original. Everything about you is unique and special. You were made especially for the man God has given you. What do I mean?

Genesis 2:18-24

18And the Lord God said, 'It is not good that man should be alone; I will make him a helper comparable to him.' 19Out of the ground the Lord God formed every beast of the field and every bird of the air, and brought them to Adam to see what he would call them. And whatever Adam called each living creature, that was its name. 20So Adam gave names to all cattle, to the birds of the air, and to every beast of the field. But for Adam there was not found a helper comparable to him. 21And the Lord God caused a deep sleep to fall on Adam, and he slept; and He took one of his ribs, and closed up the flesh in its place. 22Then the rib which the Lord God had taken from man He made into a woman, and He brought her to the man. 23And Adam said: This is now bone of my bones and flesh of my flesh: She shall be called Woman, Because she was taken out of Man. 24Therefore a man shall leave his father and mother and be joined to his wife, and thy shall become one flesh.

So you see, before your husband-to-be was made in his mother's womb, God thought of you. God made you to be your husband's helper. It is for you to help your husband spiritually and emotionally. You are to build your husband up and not tear him down. Help his dreams and desires become a reality. Help your husband by being understanding and supportive. We, as women, play an important role to our husbands and in our households as well. God says in **Proverbs 14:1:** *"The wise woman builds her house, but the foolish pulls it down with her hands."* (NIV) Then He says in **Proverbs 12:4:** *"An excellent wife is the crown of her husband, but she who causes shame is like rottenness in his bones."* (NIV)

Imagine that. You can be the crown of your husband or you can contribute to the rotting of his bones. You have the ability to make your husband happy or extremely miserable. Do not do anything that will cause shame to fall upon your husband and yourself.

Webster's dictionary provided a better understanding of the word "crown." It means *"to complete successfully; put the finishing touch on."* God is saying that an excellent wife will successfully complete her husband. She will put the finishing touches on him. You see, your husband will be strong in some areas and not as strong in others, but where he lacks you will pick up. Don't be the wife that tears her home apart. Rather, be the wife that builds her home, completes her home and fights for her home. Your fiancé is more to you than you know. He is your future. He is your future husband, the future father of your children, your future business partner and your future ministry. Be sure to make the right investment in your future.

As you begin to make your plans, you need to know that you and your fiancé will not always agree on everything. While the two of you may not agree, your response and actions can make a difference in the outcome. **Proverbs 15:1:** *"A soft answer turneth away wrath: but grievous words stir up anger."* Webster defines "grievous" as *"causing suffering; hard to bear; severe."* "Wrath" means *"intense anger; rage; fury."* The way you respond can make the difference in your fiancé's attitude and actions. Remember Proverbs 15:1 as you plan your wedding and thereafter. When your fiancé has said something you do not agree with, respond softly, do not yell and do not respond in a negative way. Throughout the planning of your wedding and for the remainder of your life, you will experience situations relating to anger, finances, health, joy, love, peace, stress and even worry, just to name a few. It is important for you to know what God's word says about some of the situations that you may encounter. The next pages are scriptures relating to the topics mentioned. Before I give you scriptures, write down your thoughts relating to the topic. Write down your current struggles regarding the particular topic and even your prayer. After you write down your thoughts and feelings, read what God says about it. Are you ready to interact?

ANGER

As you think about the word anger, what comes to your mind? Are you a person easily angered? Is your fiancé a person easily angered? What types of things make you angry? Does your fiancé know what angers you? Write your thoughts and feelings about anger, and then read what God's word says about anger.

_____

_____

_____

_____

_____

_____

_____

_____

_____

_____

_____

_____

_____

_____

_____

_____

Now that you have written down your thoughts and feelings, read what God says, and then re-read what you wrote. If you see a discrepancy, pray about it, and ask God to make it right before you get married.

GOD SAYS:

Job 5:2: *For wrath killeth the foolish man, and envy slayeth the silly one.*

Psalms 37:8: *Cease from anger, and forsake wrath: fret not thyself in any wise to do evil.*

Proverbs 6:34: *For jealousy [is] the rage of a man: therefore he will not spare in the day of vengeance.*

Proverbs 12:16: *A fool's wrath is presently known: but a prudent [man] covereth shame.*

Proverbs 14:17: *[He that is] soon angry dealeth foolishly: and a man of wicked devices is hated.*

Proverbs 14:29: *[He that is] slow to wrath [is] of great understanding: but [he that is] hasty of spirit exalteth folly.*

Proverbs 15:1: *A soft answer turneth away wrath: but grievous words stir up anger.*

Proverbs 15:18: *A wrathful man stirreth up strife: but [he that is] slow to anger appeaseth strife.*

Proverbs 16:29: *A violent man enticeth his neighbor, and leadeth him into the way [that is] not good.*

Proverbs 19:19: *A man of great wrath shall suffer punishment: for if thou deliver [him], yet thou must do it again.*

Proverbs 22:24-25: *Make no friendship with an angry man; and with a furious man thou shalt not go: Lest thou learn his ways, and get a snare to thy soul.*

Proverbs 25:28: *He that [hath] no rule over his own spirit [is like] a city [that is] broken down, [and] without walls.*

Ecclesiastes 7:9: *Be not hasty in thy spirit to be angry: for anger resteth in the bosom of fools.*

FINANCES

Okay, this is a hot topic. I have found that people do not want to talk about their finances. A lot of people do not know their true financial condition because they refuse to face the bills or the phone calls. When it comes to money, people have a tendency to get very sensitive. However, if you understand money and how God expects it to work, it will not be a hot topic for you. When you think about your finances, do you cringe? When you think about your finances as it relates to your wedding, what are your thoughts? Do you get worried? Think about your current financial situation and the previous questions, and write your thoughts.

_____

_____

_____

_____

_____

_____

_____

_____

_____

THIS IS WHAT GOD SAYS:

Psalms 37:21: *The wicked borroweth, and payeth not again: but the righteous sheweth mercy, and giveth.*

Matthew 5:42: *Give to him that asketh thee, and from him that would borrow of thee turn not thou away.*

Luke 11:4: *And forgive us our sins; for we also forgive every one that is indebted to us. And lead us not into temptation; but deliver us from evil.*

Romans 13:8: *Owe no man any thing, but to love one another: for he that loveth hath fulfilled the law.*

Deuteronomy 15:7-8: *If there be among you a poor man of one of thy brethren within any of thy gates in thy land which the Lord thy God giveth thee, thou shalt not harden thine heart, nor take thine hand from thy poor brother: But thou shalt open thine hand wide unto him, and shalt surely lend him sufficient for his need, [in that] which he wanteth.*

Deuteronomy 16:17: *Every man [shall give] as he is able, according to the blessing of the Lord thy God which he hath given thee.*

Proverbs 3:9: *Honour the Lord with thy substance, and with the firstfruits of all thine increase:*

Proverbs 28:27: *He that giveth unto the poor shall not lack: but he that hideth his eyes shall have many a curse.*

Luke 6:38: *Give, and it shall be given unto you; good measure, pressed down, and shaken together, and running over, shall men give into your bosom. For with the same measure that ye mete withal it shall be measured to you again.*

II Corinthians 9:6-7: *But this [I say], He which soweth sparingly shall reap also sparingly: and he which soweth bountifully shall reap also bountifully. Every man according as he purposeth in his heart, [so let him give]; not grudgingly, or of necessity: for God loveth a cheerful giver.*

HEALTH

Your health is very important, not only to yourself, but also to your fiancé and God. Make sure you drink at least eight 8-ounce glasses of water a day. Water is good for your body and can help keep your skin pretty, banish premenstrual bloat and even activate weight loss. What are your thoughts concerning your health? Have you experienced weight concerns? What are your eating habits that can negatively affect your weight and your health? Write down your thoughts and feelings.

_____

_____

_____

_____

_____

_____

_____

_____

_____

_____

_____

_____

GOD SAYS:

Proverbs 16:24: *Pleasant words [are as] an honeycomb, sweet to the soul, and health to the bones.*

Proverbs 17:22: *A merry heart doeth good [like] a medicine: but a broken spirit drieth the bones.*

I Timothy 4:8: *For bodily exercise profiteth little: but godliness is profitable unto all things, having promise of the life that now is, and of that which is to come.*

Jeremiah 30:17: *For I will restore health unto thee, and I will heal thee of thy wounds, saith the LORD; because they called thee an Outcast, saying, This is Zion, whom no man seeketh after.*

Jeremiah 33:6: *Behold, I will bring it health and cure, and I will cure them, and will reveal unto them the abundance of peace and truth.*

3 John 1:2: *Beloved, I wish above all things that thou mayest prosper and be in health, even as thy soul prospereth.*

Proverbs 12:18: *There is that speaketh like the piercings of a sword: but the tongue of the wise is health.*

JOY

What is joy? Webster's dictionary defines "joy" as "a very glad feeling; happiness; great pleasure; delight." While you are planning your wedding and thereafter, you are to be joyous. Every moment might not be a moment of joy, but your life and overall planning should be filled with joy. Tomorrow is not promised to you; therefore, enjoy this moment and allow it to be filled with joy. How do you feel now? How do you feel about your wedding? Do you feel the joy as defined by Webster? Write down your thoughts and feelings.

_____

_____

_____

_____

_____

_____

_____

_____

_____

_____

_____

WHAT DOES GOD SAY ABOUT JOY?

Nehemiah 8:10: *Then he said unto them, go your way, eat the fat, and drink the sweet, and send portions unto them for whom nothing is prepared: for [this] day [is] holy unto our Lord: neither be ye sorry; for the joy of the Lord is your strength.*

Psalms 2:11: *Serve the Lord with fear, and rejoice with trembling.*

Psalms 5:11: *But let all those that put their trust in thee rejoice: let them ever shout for joy, because thou defendest them: let them also that love thy name be joyful in thee.*

Psalms 16:11: *Thou wilt shew me the path of life: in they presence [is] fullness of joy; at thy right hand [there are] pleasures for evermore.*

Psalms 35:9: *And my soul shall be joyful in the Lord: it shall rejoice in his salvation.*

Psalms 126:5-6: *They that sow in tears shall reap in joy. He that goeth forth and weepeth, bearing precious seed, shall doubtless come again with rejoicing, bringing his sheaves [with him].*

Ecclesiastes 2:26: *For [God] giveth to a man that [is] good in his sight wisdom, and knowledge, and joy: but to the sinner he giveth* *travail, to gather and to heap up, that he may give to [him that is] good before God. This also [is] vanity and vexation of spirit.*

Galatians 5:22: *But the fruit of the Spirit is love, joy, peace, longsuffering, gentleness, goodness, faith.*

LOVE

Wow, love!!! *"For God so loved the world that He gave his only begotten Son that whosoever believeth in Him shall not perish but have everlasting life."* (**John 3:16**) Now that's love. God loved you so much that He gave His only son for you. When you think of love, what comes to your mind? What are your thoughts regarding love? Do you have a hard time expressing your love? Write down your thoughts and feelings regarding love.

_____

_____

_____

_____

_____

_____

_____

_____

_____

_____

_____

<u>WHAT DOES GOD SAY ABOUT LOVE?</u>

Leviticus 19:18: *Thou shalt not avenge, nor bear any grudge against the children of thy people, but thou shalt love thy neighbor as thyself: I [am] the Lord.*

Deuteronomy 6:5: *And thou shalt love the Lord thy God with all thine heart, and with all thy soul, and with all thy might.*

Deuteronomy 10:12: *And now, Israel, what doth the Lord thy God require of thee, but to fear the Lord thy God, to walk in all his ways, and to love him, and to serve the Lord thy God with all thy heart and with all they soul,*

Deuteronomy 11:1: *Therefore thou shalt love the Lord thy God, and keep his charge, and his statutes, and his judgements, and his commandments, always.*

Psalms 37:4: *Delight thyself also in the Lord; and he shall give thee the desires of thine heart.*

Psalms 145:20: *The Lord preserveth all them that love him: but all the wicked will he destroy.*

Proverbs 8:17: *I love them that love me; and those that seek me early shall find me.*

Proverbs 10:12: *Hatred stirreth up strifes: but love covereth all sins.*

Proverbs 17:17: *A friend loveth at all times, and a brother is born for adversity.*

John 14:15: *If ye love me, keep my commandments.*

Ephesians 4:32: *And by ye kind one to another, tenderhearted, forgiving one another, even as God for Christ's sake hath forgiven you.*

PEACE

In all that you do, you should feel peace. There should not be one moment in which you are stressed about a decision or a situation. How are you feeling now? When you think of your life and what you have to do concerning the wedding, are you at peace? Write down your thoughts and feelings as it relates to peace in your life.

_____

_____

_____

_____

_____

_____

_____

_____

_____

_____

_____

_____

_____

NOW, THIS IS WHAT GOD SAYS ABOUT PEACE:

Job 22:21: *Acquaint now thyself with him, and be at peace: thereby good shall come unto thee.*

Psalms 29:11: *The Lord will give strength unto his people; the Lord will bless his people with peace.*

Psalms 34:14: *Depart from evil, and do good; seek peace, and pursue it.*

Psalms 37:4: *Delight thyself also in the Lord; and he shall give thee the desires of thine heart.*

Psalms 37:11: *But the meek shall inherit the earth; and shall delight themselves in the abundance of peace.*

Psalms 37:37: *Mark the perfect [man], and behold the upright: for the end of [that] man [is] peace.*

Proverbs 3:17: *Her ways [are] ways of pleasantness, and all her paths [are] peace.*

Proverbs 12:20: *Deceit [is] in the heart of them that imagine evil: but to the counsellors of peace [is] joy.*

Proverbs 16:7: *When a man's ways please the Lord, he maketh even his enemies to be at peace with him.*

Isaiah 6:3: *Thou wilt keep [him] in perfect peace, [whose] mind [is] stayed [on thee]: because he trusteth in thee.*

Matthew 5:9: *Blessed [are] the peacemakers: for they shall be called the children of God.*

John 16:33: *These things I have spoken unto you, that in me ye might have peace. In the world ye shall have tribulation: but be of good cheer; I have overcome the world.*

Romans 12:18: *If it be possible, as much as lieth in you, live peaceably with all men.*

Romans 14:19: *Let us therefore follow after the things which make for peace, and things wherewith one may edify another.*

I Corinthians 14:33: *For God is not [the author] of confusion, but of peace, as in all churches of the saints.*

STRESS

Stress is something that everyone faces at one time or another. However, stress can affect one's life span. It is important to your health to relieve stress or prevent it from becoming too severe. Whether you realize it or not, your attitude plays a big part in the stress levels you may experience. Do not allow yourself to dwell on negative thoughts or past events. Do you find yourself frequently stressed? What activities do you engage in to relieve your stress? Write down your thoughts regarding stress.

_____

_____

_____

_____

_____

_____

_____

_____

_____

_____

_____

_____

Now, that you have written your thoughts concerning stress, this is what God says:

Psalms 18:3-6: *I will call upon the Lord, [who is worthy] to be praised: so shall I be saved from mine enemies. The sorrows of death compassed me, and the floods of ungodly men made me afraid. The sorrows of hell compassed me about: the snares of death prevented me. In my distress I called upon the Lord, and cried unto my God: he heard my voice out of his temple, and my cry came before him, [even] into his ears.*

Psalms 55:22: *Cast thy burden upon the Lord, and he shall sustain thee: he shall never suffer the righteous to be moved.*

Psalms 56:3-4: *What time I am afraid, I will trust in thee. In God I will praise his word, in God I have put my trust; I will not fear what flesh can do unto me.*

Psalms 118:5-9: *I called upon the Lord in distress: the Lord answered me, [and set me] in a large place. The Lord [is] on my side; I will not fear: what can man do unto me? The Lord taketh my part with them that help me: therefore shall I see [my desire] upon them that hate me. [It is] better to trust in the Lord than to put*

*confidence in man. [It is] better to trust in the
Lord than to put confidence in princes.*

If you are a person who is easily stressed, here are some ideas on de-stressing.

- Take a warm bath with lighted candles and soft music.

- Make up your bed, fluff your pillows, get a hot cup of tea or cocoa, climb in bed and watch your favorite movie.

- Schedule a fun time with the girls. Call your girlfriends for a night of pizza and laughs. This will definitely change your mood.

Don't think that you have to be stressed while planning your wedding. If you feel yourself getting overwhelmed, take an evening off. Make the decision that, at least one night a week, you will schedule a time for you. Set aside the wedding plans and discussions, and use this time to relax and enjoy life.

WORRY

Worry changes nothing!!! If you have not learned this already, you will. Sometimes we allow ourselves to become worried about money, bills, weight, work, etc. However, while we are worrying, the situation is not changing. Do you find yourself worrying about things? What do you do when you worry about an issue? Has your situation changed as a result of your worrying? Think about these questions and write down your feelings and thoughts below.

_____

_____

_____

_____

_____

_____

_____

_____

_____

_____

_____

_____

_____

SO, WHAT DOES GOD SAY ABOUT WORRYING?

Matthew 6:25-33: *Therefore I say unto you, Take no thought for your life, what ye shall eat, or what ye shall drink; nor yet for your body, what ye shall put on. Is not the life more than meat, and the body than raiment? Behold the fowls of the air: for they sow not, neither do they reap, nor gather into barns; yet your heavenly Father feedeth them. Are ye not much better than they? Which of you by taking thought can add one cubit unto his stature? And why take ye thought for raiment? Consider the lilies of the field, how they grow; they toil not, neither do they spin: And yet I say unto you, That even Solomon in all his glory was not arrayed like one of these. Wherefore, if God so clothe the grass of the field, which to day is, and tomorrow is cast into the oven, [shall he] not much more [clothe] you, O ye of little faith? Therefore take no thought, saying, What shall we eat? Or, What shall we drink? Or, Wherewithal shall we be clothed? (For after all these things do the Gentiles seek:) for your heavenly Father knoweth that ye have need of all these things. But seek ye first the kingdom of God, and his righteousness; and all these things shall be added unto you.*

Philippians 4:6: *Be careful for nothing; but in every thing by prayer and supplication with* *thanksgiving let your request be made known unto God.*

I Peter 5:7: *Casting all your care upon him; for he careth for you.*

Section Three

PLANNING PAGES

Bride: _____

Groom: _____

Wedding Date: _____

Matron of Honor: _____

Maid of Honor: _____

Best Man: _____

Wedding Coordinator: _____

Ring Bearer: _____

Flower Girl: _____

Bridesmaids: _____

_____

_____

Groomsmen: _____

_____

_____

_____

_____

A LETTER TO THE BRIDE

This is an exciting time for you. You are about to plan one of the most important events of your life — the wedding of your dreams. Despite the challenges that may come your way, remember the words that were written earlier in this book. Use this book and the contents therein as a guide and as your personal support. While you have a lot to plan, do not miss out on a moment. Years from now, I want you to be able to pull out this book and reflect on your experiences.

This planner will assist you in maintaining your schedule, and it will allow you to express your feelings as you experience each event. This planner provides a systematic guide that you will find very useful.

I speak the blessings of the Lord over you. I pray your planning is stress-free and fun and that your wedding day is flawless. I further pray that your love lasts forever and that your marriage is an example for others to follow.

Be blessed,

Tania White

GETTING THE WORD OUT

One of my best memories is the reactions I received when I informed my family and friends that Maurice and I were getting married. I had talked about marrying Maurice for years to anyone who would listen. The supportive outbursts of emotions and tears from my family and friends only added to my joy. The first reaction is usually a reflection of the true feelings someone has regarding your news. Regardless of the reactions of others, just know that if God has brought you two together, then that is all that matters. Don't expect everyone to share your sentiments. If you meet with negativity, simply smile and pray that their feelings do not interfere with God's plans for you.

Okay, now is the time. Think back and write down your first wedding experiences. Years down the line when you read about the reactions of your family and friends, it will bring that moment back to you in such a great way. So, get to writing.

Who was the first person you told? _____

How did you tell them? _____

What was his/her response? _____

Was it the response you expected? _____

Who was the first friend you told? _____

How did your mother react? _____

_____

    As you reflect on the moment you got engaged and the moments when you informed your family and friends, what thoughts run through your mind? How do you feel? Use this page to write down your thoughts and feelings of the reactions you received. As you reflect, you might want to answer the following questions. How did their reactions make you feel? How did you feel before you told your family and friends, and how did you feel after you told them? Did you get the responses you expected? Whose response was most surprising? By asking yourself these previous questions, you will allow yourself to record your deepest feelings concerning the first phase of your engagement.

    I have told my friends and family that I am engaged to _____ and these are my feelings regarding their responses:

_____

_____

_____

_____

_____

_____

_____

_____

_____

_____

_____

_____

_____

Now you have gotten through the first step of your engagement, which is telling everyone. Your next step will be communication. You may say, "I just communicated by telling my family and friends I am engaged." You are right, but you now need to communicate with your fiancé about the wedding details before any official wedding planning begins. It is important that both you and your fiancé have an understanding of what type and size wedding you anticipate. Before you speak with your fiancé regarding the details of the wedding, be sure to pray. Ask God to guide you through your conversations. One topic that usually stirs any individual is the subject of money. Before you discuss any financial concerns and responsibilities you need to ask God to come in and allow His will to be done. When it comes to spending money, some people are irrational and others are over-rational. Women sometimes think that the wedding is all about them, and that the men are supposed to merely show up. I bind that thinking right now. The wedding day is just as important to a man as it is to a woman. Do not allow yourself to neglect your fiancé and his ideas. Include him in the decision-making process. Remember, it is his wedding day too.

As the two of you sit down to discuss the intricate details of the wedding, there are a couple of things you should do.

1.   Open the meeting with prayer. Ask God to come in, have His way in your planning session, and guide your decisions.

2.   Stand on this scripture: **Proverbs 15:1:** *"A gentle answer turns away wrath, But a harsh word stirs up anger."* Regardless of any opposition on the part of your fiancé, please remember Proverbs 15:1; it will make a difference. There may be moments in which your fiancé may even raise his voice to get a point across. It is imperative that you do not respond likewise, but rather with a soft answer. When you provide a soft answer to an

irate or upset person, you will cause his attitude to change, and eventually he may become less irate and more rational.

3.   Take notes. The process of organizing a wedding can become an important lesson in working together towards a common goal. You and your husband will have to work together on many issues concerning your life together. The more you explore your options together, the more you learn about each other's preferences, priorities and tastes. The more you learn, the better the decisions you will be able to make.

One of the first discussions between you and your fiancé should pertain to the size of the wedding. This can be done by completing a tentative guest list. You and your fiancé should write names of tentative guests and decide if you want them to attend both the wedding and reception. Once your lists are completed, you and your fiancé should meet and discuss the lists. Some changes may or may not be made, but the two of you will have a clear understanding of the expected size of your wedding, which will then lead to other decisions that will need to be made.

The next couple of pages are for your tentative guest list. It is a good idea to start with categories and then list names. (e.g., family, sorority sisters, college friends and co-workers) Write down the categories of everyone you think that you may want to invite to your wedding, and have your fiancé do the same. Upon completion of your categories, make a name list. The two of you should come back together to discuss your numbers. Remember, this may not be your final list.

TENTATIVE GUEST LIST

_____

_____

_____

_____

_____

_____

_____

_____

_____

_____

_____

_____

_____

_____

_____

_____

_____

_____

_____

_____

_____

Tania A. White

Tania A. White

90

"So, You're Engaged?"

_____

_____

_____

_____

_____

_____

_____

_____

_____

_____

_____

_____

_____

_____

_____

_____

_____

_____

_____

_____

_____

_____

Tania A. White

"So, You're Engaged?"

_____

_____

_____

_____

_____

_____

_____

_____

_____

_____

_____

_____

_____

_____

_____

_____

_____

_____

_____

_____

_____

_____

_____

Tania A. White

"So, You're Engaged?"

WEDDING RINGS

Now that you have consolidated your lists, it is time for you to begin looking for your fiancé's ring. It is important that you pick the ring you want for your fiancé with the understanding that he is entitled to input. Don't show him the ring, but do consult him on his taste so that he will love his ring as much as you love yours. Don't be in a hurry to purchase a ring. Selections can include rubies, diamonds, emeralds, etc. If you decide to pick a diamond, then you should understand the elements that determine a diamond's quality, this way you will have a better chance of getting the best diamond for your money. Based upon my research, I learned that there are four classic criteria when selecting a diamond: color, cut, clarity and carat. The color, cut and clarity determine the price per carat. Once that is established, carat weight determines the final price.

So, what are color, cut, clarity and carat? "Color" refers to the clearness of the diamond. The clearer the diamond, the greater its value. I learned that diamonds are graded on a scale. The greater the degree of the color of a stone, then the lower the stone's value will be, with the exception of very rare colored diamonds, which are extremely valuable. Clear or colorless stones are considered to be perfect.

Use the chart below when picking your diamond to measure your grade.

D	E	F	G	H	I	J	K	L	M	N	O	P	Q	R	S	T	U	V	W	X	Y	Z	FANCY LIGHT	FANCY INTENSE
Colorless			Near Colorless				Faint Yellow			Very Light Yellow					Light Yellow								Fancy Yellow	

"Cut" refers to the shape of the diamond. Cut is important because it is essential to the beauty and sparkle of the diamond. The brilliant or round cut is the most common. Other diamond shapes are oval, pear, marquise, emerald, and heart-shaped. "Clarity" is the degree of inclusions (interior or exterior flaws) when the stone is magnified ten times. If the inclusions are large and noticeable without a magnifying glass, they will affect the beauty and the value of the stone. Flawless or perfect stones are stones without any imperfections. Finally, "Carat" refers to the size of the diamond. Color, cut and clarity determine the per carat value of the diamond. A higher quality, smaller diamond will be worth more than a lower quality, larger diamond.

When you make the decision to purchase your ring, be sure you deal with a reliable, reputable jeweler. Know the budget you have to work with before you begin to shop. Also, shop around, and compare several rings from different jewelers. Do not limit yourself to just one store. You may be able to find a better deal if you shop around.

Questions for the Jeweler:

How long have you been in business? _____

What services does your store offer (e.g., cleaning, sizing, engraving, remounting)? _____

_____

_____

Does the store have an upgrade policy? If so, what is it?

_____

_____

_____

Is there a re-sizing chart? How long does re-sizing take?

_____

_____

_____

What is the store's return policy? _____

_____

_____

99

What is the policy for repairs, tightening of the stone and cleaning? _____

Use the next page to document information as you search for that special ring. _____

_____

_____

_____

_____

_____

_____

_____

_____

_____

_____

_____

_____

JEWELRY WORKSHEET

	Estimate #1	Estimate #2	Estimate #3	Estimate #4
Jewelry Store				
Location/ Phone				
Size (number of carats)				
Cut (shape of stone)				
Color (grade)				
Price				

Jeweler Choice

Name: _____

Address: _____

Phone: _____

Salesperson: _____

Total Cost: _____ Deposit Paid: _____

Balance Due: _____ Pickup Date: _____

Other Notes: _____

_____

_____

_____

_____

PLANNING CALENDAR

Planning is essential to any major event. While you may know the intricate details of your wedding, it will not flow smoothly without adequate planning. One of the first steps to ensure effective planning is to allow for ample time. Do not wait until the last minute. Initially, you must determine the time of year for your wedding. This might be a special date or season. The date also will be a factor when planning your honeymoon. If there is a place that you have always dreamed about for your honeymoon, you may want to pick the best date and plan your wedding around that date. Nevertheless, be sure to consult your fiancé before making too many plans.

The following checklist and calendar are provided for you and your fiancé to organize your planning and to get a handle on all aspects of your wedding. Do not assume that your fiancé has taken care of his portion; keep the communication open.

BRIDE'S CHECKLIST

Six to Twelve Months Before:

❑ Select a wedding date and time.

❑ Make a preliminary budget.

❑ Make a tentative guest list.

❑ Determine your wedding theme or style.

❑ Reserve your ceremony and reception locations.

❑ Determine who will officiate the ceremony.

❑ Decide who your wedding consultant will be.

❑ Decide upon the color scheme.

❑ Finalize the guest list.

❑ After you have prayed, select bridal attendants.

❑ Have your fiancé select his attendants.

❑ Plan reception.

❑ Check catering facilities. Be sure to check hotels; you can really get a good rate.

❑ Select a photographer and videographer.

❏ Select a florist.

❏ Select your dress and headpiece.

❏ Select bridesmaids' dresses.

❏ Make transportation arrangements for the wedding day.

Four Months Before:

❏ Make final arrangements for ceremony. All deposits should be paid and contracts signed.

❏ Make sure necessary bridal attire is ordered.

❏ Discuss the color scheme with both mothers. Have them to coordinate and select their dresses.

❏ Register at a bridal registry.

❏ Order invitations and personal stationery.

❏ Complete guest lists, and put them in order.

❏ Check requirements for marriage license and passports.

❏ Start to plan the honeymoon.

❏ Decide where you will live after the wedding.

❏ Begin making appointments to view homes.

Two Months Before:

❑ Address invitations and announcements, they are typically mailed 4 to 6 weeks before the wedding.

❑ Finalize all details with caterer, photographer, florist, musician, and reception hall.

❑ Finalize ceremony details with Officiant.

❑ Make rehearsal arrangements.

❑ Plan rehearsal dinner.

❑ Make appointment with hairdresser. You should schedule two appointments. The first should be a test run and the second should be for the wedding.

❑ Arrange accommodations for out-of-town guests, and communicate information.

❑ Finalize honeymoon plans.

One Month Before:

❑ Have your final fitting.

❑ Have a final fitting for your bridesmaids.

❑ Get marriage license.

❑ Select responsible people to handle wishing well, guest book and gifts.

Two Weeks Before:

☐ Attend to business and legal details. Get all necessary forms to change names on your Social Security card, driver's license, and insurance and medical plans.

☐ Reconfirm the accommodations for out-of-town guests.

☐ Begin the process of moving to your new home. Give a change of address card to the post office.

☐ Schedule a taste testing for meal and cake.

One Week Before:

☐ Contact guests who have not responded. This is a courtesy to make sure they received the invitation.

☐ Give the final count to the caterer or reception hall.

☐ Go over the final details with the videographer, photographer and florist.

☐ Provide photographer with a list of pictures you want.

☐ Provide the videographer a list of shots you would like included in the video.

☐ Give all musicians the lists of the music.

☐ Plan the seating arrangements.

❑ Arrange for someone to assist you with last minute details.

❑ Decide who will help you dress.

❑ Practice your makeup in the same type of lighting.

❑ Pack your suitcase for the honeymoon.

❑ Make sure you have your marriage license.

❑ Make sure you have the wedding rings.

❑ Make sure all wedding attire is picked up and that it fits.

❑ Have a rehearsal the night before.

❑ Attend rehearsal dinner and have fun.

On the Wedding Day:

❑ Be sure to eat!!! We don't want you fainting.

❑ Be calm, smile and get ready for a day of history.

❑ Make sure you have all of your accessories.

❑ Bring makeup, lotion, deodorant, breathmints, and Kleenex.

❑ Don't allow anyone or anything to ruin your day or upset you. Remember, this is your day and your memories. Make sure your memories are worth remembering. No one is more important than you and your fiancé.

After the Wedding:

❑ Enjoy your honeymoon.

❑ Be sure to take lots of pictures and relax.

❑ Write and mail thank-you notes.

MONTHLY PLANNING CALENDAR

Month: _____ Months until big day: _____

1		17	
2		18	
3		19	
4		20	
5		21	
6		22	
7		23	
8		24	
9		25	
10		26	
11		27	
12		28	
13		29	
14		30	
15		31	
16			

Notes: _____

_____

_____

_____

_____

_____

MONTHLY PLANNING CALENDAR

Month: _____ Months until big day: _____

1		17	
2		18	
3		19	
4		20	
5		21	
6		22	
7		23	
8		24	
9		25	
10		26	
11		27	
12		28	
13		29	
14		30	
15		31	
16			

Notes: _____

_____

_____

_____

_____

MONTHLY PLANNING CALENDAR

Month: _____ Months until big day: _____

1		17	
2		18	
3		19	
4		20	
5		21	
6		22	
7		23	
8		24	
9		25	
10		26	
11		27	
12		28	
13		29	
14		30	
15		31	
16			

Notes: _____

_____

_____

_____

_____

MONTHLY PLANNING CALENDAR

Month: _____ Months until big day: _____

1		17	
2		18	
3		19	
4		20	
5		21	
6		22	
7		23	
8		24	
9		25	
10		26	
11		27	
12		28	
13		29	
14		30	
15		31	
16			

Notes: _____

_____

_____

_____

_____

MONTHLY PLANNING CALENDAR

Month: _____ Months until big day: _____

1		17	
2		18	
3		19	
4		20	
5		21	
6		22	
7		23	
8		24	
9		25	
10		26	
11		27	
12		28	
13		29	
14		30	
15		31	
16			

Notes: _____

_____

_____

_____

_____

MONTHLY PLANNING CALENDAR

Month: _____ Months until big day: _____

1		17	
2		18	
3		19	
4		20	
5		21	
6		22	
7		23	
8		24	
9		25	
10		26	
11		27	
12		28	
13		29	
14		30	
15		31	
16			

Notes: _____

_____

_____

_____

_____

_____

MONTHLY PLANNING CALENDAR

Month: _____ Months until big day: _____

1		17	
2		18	
3		19	
4		20	
5		21	
6		22	
7		23	
8		24	
9		25	
10		26	
11		27	
12		28	
13		29	
14		30	
15		31	
16			

Notes: _____

_____

_____

_____

_____

_____

Tania A. White

MONTHLY PLANNING CALENDAR

Month: _____ Months until big day: _____

1		17	
2		18	
3		19	
4		20	
5		21	
6		22	
7		23	
8		24	
9		25	
10		26	
11		27	
12		28	
13		29	
14		30	
15		31	
16			

Notes: _____

_____

_____

_____

_____

MONTHLY PLANNING CALENDAR

Month: _____ Months until big day: _____

1		17	
2		18	
3		19	
4		20	
5		21	
6		22	
7		23	
8		24	
9		25	
10		26	
11		27	
12		28	
13		29	
14		30	
15		31	
16			

Notes: _____

_____

_____

_____

_____

MONTHLY PLANNING CALENDAR

Month: _____ Months until big day: _____

1		17	
2		18	
3		19	
4		20	
5		21	
6		22	
7		23	
8		24	
9		25	
10		26	
11		27	
12		28	
13		29	
14		30	
15		31	
16			

Notes: _____

_____

_____

_____

_____

MONTHLY PLANNING CALENDAR

Month: _____ Months until big day: _____

1		17	
2		18	
3		19	
4		20	
5		21	
6		22	
7		23	
8		24	
9		25	
10		26	
11		27	
12		28	
13		29	
14		30	
15		31	
16			

Notes: _____

_____

_____

_____

_____

_____

MONTHLY PLANNING CALENDAR

Month: _____ Months until big day: _____

1		17	
2		18	
3		19	
4		20	
5		21	
6		22	
7		23	
8		24	
9		25	
10		26	
11		27	
12		28	
13		29	
14		30	
15		31	
16			

Notes: _____

_____

_____

_____

_____

_____

MONTHLY PLANNING CALENDAR

Month: _____ Months until big day: _____

1		17	
2		18	
3		19	
4		20	
5		21	
6		22	
7		23	
8		24	
9		25	
10		26	
11		27	
12		28	
13		29	
14		30	
15		31	
16			

Notes: _____

_____

_____

_____

_____

INFORMATION WORKSHEET

Ceremony Location: _____

_____

Date: _____

Ceremony Address: _____

Phone: _____

Restrictions: _____

Rehearsal Date: _____ Time: _____

Number of guests: _____

Number in wedding party: _____

Wedding Colors: _____

Is there an area to dress for the bride, groom and attendants?

_____

_____

Reception Location: _____

_____

Phone: _____

Reception Address: _____

_____

Reservation Time: _____

Officiant: _____ Phone: _____

Soloist: _____ Phone: _____

Photographer: _____ Phone: _____

Videographer: _____ Phone: _____

Florist: _____ Phone: _____

Bakery: _____ Phone: _____

Musician: _____ Phone: _____

Caterer: _____ Phone: _____

Special Notes: _____

_____

_____

_____

_____

_____

_____

_____

_____

_____

_____

_____

_____

_____

_____

_____

"So, You're Engaged?"

_____

_____

_____

_____

_____

_____

_____

_____

_____

_____

_____

_____

_____

_____

_____

_____

_____

_____

_____

_____

_____

_____

_____

"So, You're Engaged?"

THE PLANNING IS OVER

You have planned your heart out, and now it is time for you to enjoy. Enjoy being the center of attention, enjoy your new husband, and enjoy your new home. You and your new husband are all that matter. All the planning that you have done, all the phone calls, and all the meetings were for this one special day of memories that will last a lifetime. Use today as an opportunity to share laughs with not only your friends and family, but also the friends and family of your new husband as well.

Bride, enjoy this day and the days to come. I speak that no weapon formed against your marriage shall prosper. I speak that you shall have fullness of joy within your life and your marriage. Love your husband dearly, and do not allow anyone to come between you, but allow God to be before you. Keep God first, and you will not go wrong. With God at the helm guiding you every step of the way, you will make it through.

Now, go get some rest!! You have a beautiful wedding to attend. Be sure to relax and enjoy every moment.

Best Wishes,

Tania White

For more information

or to contact

Tania A. White

Please e-mail, write or visit her website:

P.O. Box 16634

Chicago, Illinois 60616

Tele: (888) 713-0098

E-mail: TaniaWhite03@yahoo.com

www.TaniaWhite.com

Lightning Source UK Ltd.
Milton Keynes UK
UKOW06f2350270616

277220UK00016B/587/P

9 780979 045042